HORSEPOWER

HELICOPTERS

by Martha E. H. Rustad

Reading Consultant:

Barbara J. Fox

Reading Specialist

North Carolina State University

Content Consultant:

Gregory P. Kennedy, Executive Director

American Helicopter Museum & Education Center

West Chester, Pennsylvania

Capstone
press®

Mankato, Minnesota

Blazers is published by Capstone Press,
151 Good Counsel Drive, P.O. Box 669, Mankato, Minnesota 56002.
www.capstonepress.com

Library of Congress Cataloging-in-Publication Data
Rustad, Martha E. H. (Martha Elizabeth Hillman), 1975–
    Helicopters / by Martha E. H. Rustad.
    p. cm.—(Blazers. Horsepower)
    Summary: "Describes helicopters, their main features, and how
they are used"—Provided by publisher.
    Includes bibliographical references and index.
    ISBN-13: 978-1-4296-0828-2 (hardcover)
    ISBN-10: 1-4296-0828-5 (hardcover)
    1. Helicopters—Juvenile literature. I. Title.
TL716.R77 2008
629.133'352—dc22   2007005408

Editorial Credits
Christopher L. Harbo, editor; Jason Knudson, set designer; Patrick D.
    Dentinger, book designer; Jo Miller, photo researcher

Photo Credits
AP/Wide World Photos/Mark J. Terrill, 21
Corbis/Jack Novak, 24–25
Photo by Ted Carlson/Fotodynamics, cover, 4–5, 6–7, 8–9, 10–11,
    12, 20, 26–27, 28–29
Photri-MicroStock, 22–23
Shutterstock/David Hancock, 18–19; Nicholas Rjabow, 14–15;
    Stas Volik, 16–17; Terry Poche, 13
U.S. Navy Photo by PH2 Robert M Schalk, 24

1 2 3 4 5 6 12 11 10 09 08 07

TABLE OF CONTENTS

OCEAN RESCUE

A rescue helicopter's rotors pound the heliport with gusts of air. The helicopter lifts off. The pilot and crew head out for an ocean rescue.

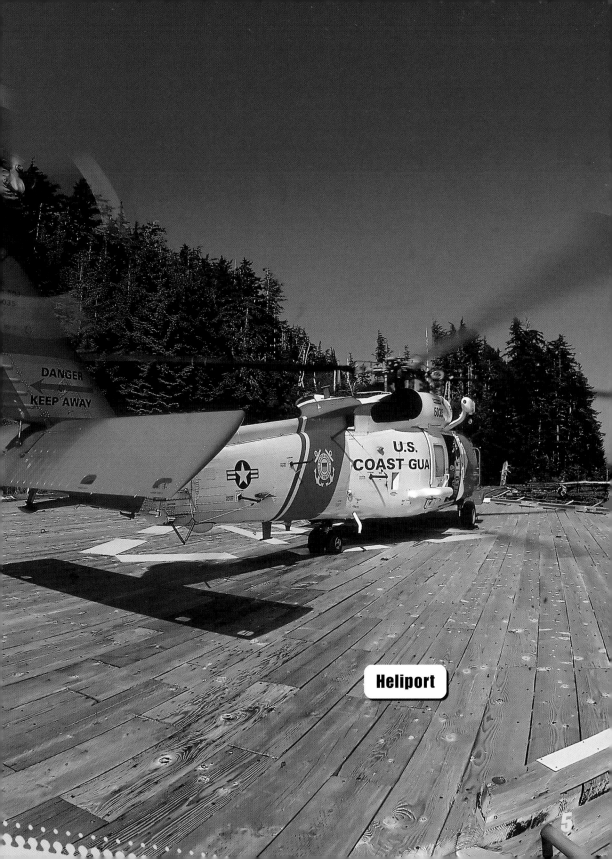

DANGER
KEEP AWAY

U.S.
COAST GUA

6036

Heliport

5

The chopper hovers over the water. The crew lowers a basket at the end of a long cable. The helicopter carries the boaters to safety.

BLAZER FACT

Helicopter nicknames include chopper, eggbeater, and whirlybird.

Helicopters do much more than rescue missions. They quickly move both people and cargo. Some helicopters have guns for military attack missions.

BLAZER FACT

Helicopters fly forward, backward, up, down, and sideways.

HELICOPTER DESIGN

Helicopters can take off and land in tight spaces. They also fly at lower speeds and closer to the ground than airplanes.

Main rotor

Tail rotor

The main rotor on top lifts the helicopter off the ground. A tail rotor at the back helps the chopper turn and fly straight ahead.

The Chinook is a twin-rotor helicopter. It has two main rotors, one on each end of the chopper.

Chinook

Lightweight engines power helicopters. These engines help helicopters fly at speeds up to 175 miles (280 kilometers) per hour.

HELICOPTER PARTS

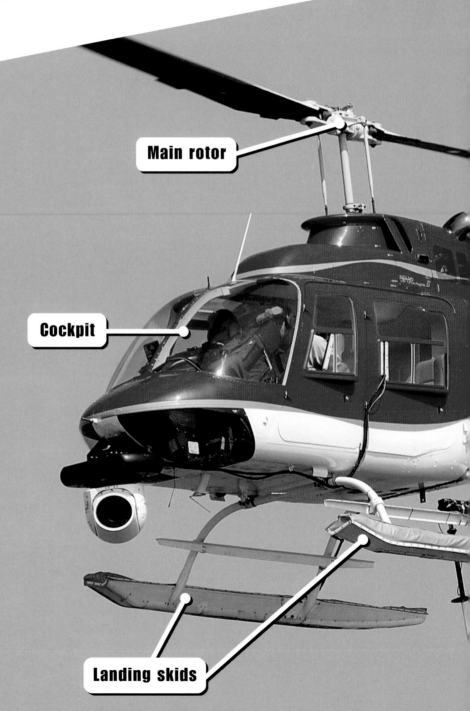

Main rotor

Cockpit

Landing skids

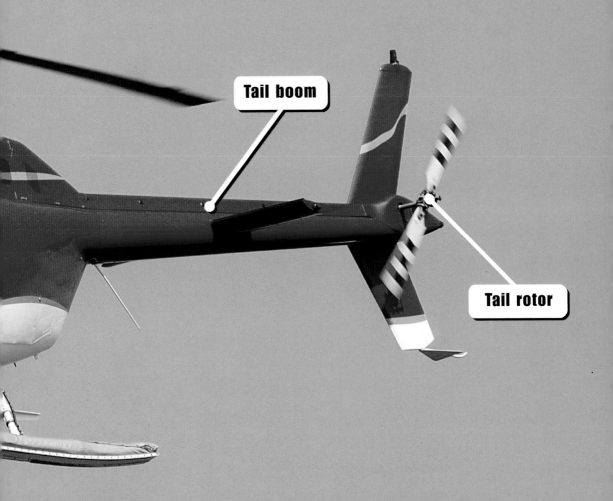

Tail boom

Tail rotor

HELICOPTERS IN ACTION

People use helicopters for many jobs. Medical helicopters carry accident victims to hospitals. Pilots in traffic helicopters watch for traffic jams on highways.

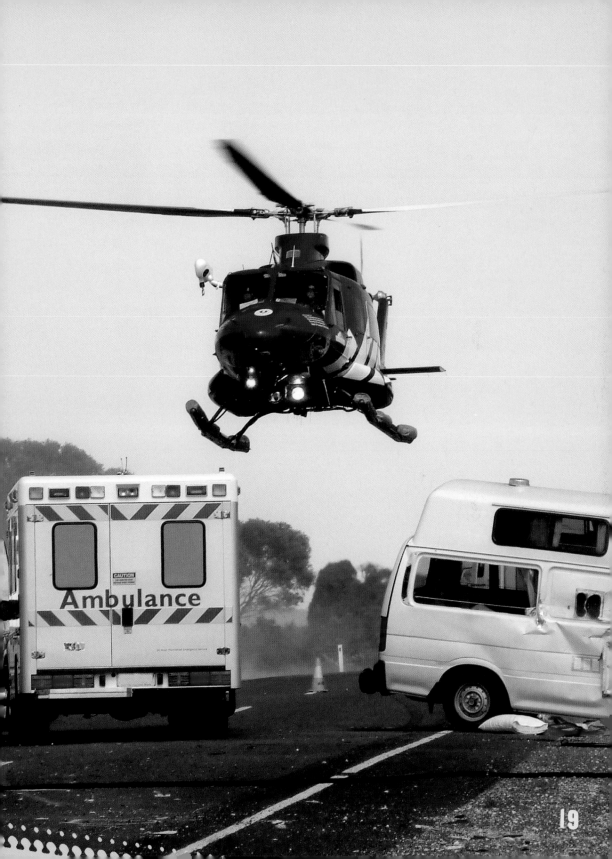

Military helicopters move troops
and supplies. Helicopters also bring
food and medicine to flood victims.

BLAZER FACT

Firefighters use helicopters to suck water out of lakes and dump it on raging forest fires.

FAMOUS HELICOPTERS

Helicopters carry people from airports to heliports in big cities. The U.S. president travels on a helicopter called Marine One.

The U.S. Army uses the Apache as an attack helicopter. Apaches carry missiles, rockets, and machine guns.

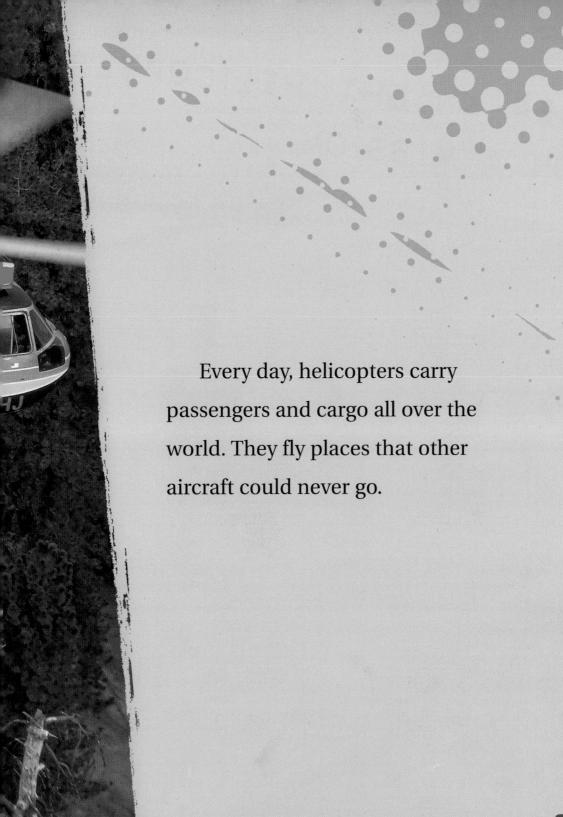

Every day, helicopters carry passengers and cargo all over the world. They fly places that other aircraft could never go.

SEA KNIGHT HELICOPTERS ON A MISSION

GLOSSARY

cable (KAY-buhl)—a thick wire or rope

cargo (KAR-goh)—objects carried by an aircraft, ship, or other vehicle

cockpit (KOK-pit)—the area in a helicopter where the pilot sits

heliport (HEL-uh-port)—a landing or takeoff place for a helicopter

hover (HUHV-ur)—to remain in one place in the air

missile (MISS-uhl)—an explosive weapon that can fly long distances

mission (MISH-uhn)—a military task

rotor (ROH-tur)—a set of rotating blades that lifts an aircraft off the ground

READ MORE

Bender, Lionel. *Airplanes and Helicopters.*
On the Move. North Mankato, Minn.:
Chrysalis Education, 2006.

Eden, Paul E. *Helicopters.* Aircraft of the World.
Milwaukee: Gareth Stevens, 2006.

Zuehlke, Jeffrey. *Helicopters.* Pull Ahead Books.
Minneapolis: Lerner, 2005.

INTERNET SITES

FactHound offers a safe, fun way to find Internet sites
related to this book. All of the sites on FactHound have
been researched by our staff.

Here's how:

1. Visit *www.facthound.com*
2. Choose your grade level.
3. Type in this special code **1429608285** for
   age-appropriate sites. You may also browse
   subjects by clicking on letters, or by clicking
   on pictures and words.
4. Click on the **Fetch It** button.

FactHound will fetch the best sites for you!

INDEX